GREEN MAN

• Jeremy Harte •

This Green Man in Norwich Cathedral, in Norfolk, is in the style called 'the foliate head', in which the shape of the face changes imperceptibly into leaves. Villard de Honnecourt, the 13th-century master mason who kept a notebook of designs, calls this the tête de feuilles. The most ingenious form of this design is the leaf mask, in which the face is composed entirely of leaves, curled and crisped to resemble human features, perhaps with eyes and a mouth added.

The decoration in the crypt at Canterbury Cathedral, in Kent was inspired by contemporary manuscripts. These cat-masks sprouting beaded interlace were carved by the French masons who arrived, with the stone they worked, from Caen in the 11th century. In the same place, later work of the 12th century, in which the foliage begins to look more like real leaves, was introduced by craftsmen who came over from Sens with William the Master Mason.

Like the earlier Celtic carvings, medieval heads appear on boundaries and crossing places. This is why Green Men can usually be found beside the church door, or at the point of transition from holy to most holy – the chancel arch. This head flanks the door at the richly decorated church of Kilpeck, in Herefordshire. Despite their barbaric pagan look, the carvings are a sophisticated version of art from the pilgrims' route to Spain and were carved in the 1140s.

GREEN MEN do not appear in England until the twelfth century, but they have a long history elsewhere. During the first century AD, decorative artists in Imperial Rome developed a playful tradition in which little people were seen hiding among leaves, turning into leaves or actually being formed from them. Foliate heads of this kind were produced as ornaments on temple friezes and capitals throughout the Roman Empire, from Turkey to the Rhine. Both foliate and sprouting heads also appear in Indian art from the eighth century, long before they became common in Europe.

It is quite demanding to carve a realistic face formed out of leaves, and the sculptors, in the later years of the western Roman Empire, when they were producing much cruder work, hit on the idea of making the leaves come out, like tendrils, from an otherwise human face. The first European example of these sprouting heads appears on the tomb of St Abre, near the city of Poitiers, in France. Later on, the same area of France saw the development of Green Man carvings in Gothic style.

Traditions which portrayed a human face among leaves were already old in northern Europe when the Romans invaded. Celtic art is based on complicated curved and twisting forms, resembling the growth of vegetation. Sometimes these forms are also adapted to suggest the bodies of animals or the heads of men, and there are designs which could be plants and human heads at the same time. The tradition died out when the Romans invaded Gaul, but it continued to imbue artists with a feeling for leaf patterns.

Many of the early Green Men were copied from illuminated manuscripts. The interlaced patterns in these books portray a tangled and frightening world, where people are lost in vegetation and things no longer have clear forms, everything turning into something else. Their faces are often flat and anonymous; character was introduced later on.

After 1200, the whole character of Green Men, like other carvings of leaves and flowers, seems to change. At first the sprouting heads are still set in rows or circles, as if their individuality doesn't matter very much, but later they start to look more like real people. The tendrils of the foliage also start to look more realistic, like these hop leaves framing a face in the chapter house at Wells Cathedral, in Somerset.

Little heads of dragons and cats bite at the foliage in manuscripts of the 10th century onwards. Cat-masks, with two strands of foliage going into their ears and coming out of their mouths, were copied in sculpture and influenced many of the early Green Men. On this font at Lullington church, in Somerset, a ring of four cats' heads sprouts foliage above a Latin inscription which translates as: 'In this holy bowl sins are washed from the soul'.

Although the Green Man is often associated with the hawthorn, or May tree, if you look more closely at the carvings, you will see that he is an emblem of autumn, not of spring. The hawthorn leaves are never accompanied by flowers, but often by fruit. At the church of Sutton Benger, Wiltshire, the generous Green Man provides hawthorn berries for the birds. The crudest carver could usually manage to surround him with some acorns or grapes.

OLD CHURCHES can seem very stark and plain today, but in the Middle Ages they would have been bright with green and gold, the colours of growth. Medieval people loved bright colours, which were so difficult for them to make artificially and yet so abundant in nature. The mystic, Hildegarde of Bingen, spoke of *viriditas,* 'the green-ing of the soul'. The Green Man would have conjured up thoughts like this. He himself was always human colour, not tinted green, although there were other outlandish figures in popular tradition who were this colour. In the twelfth century, two Green Children were found at Woolpit, in Suffolk. They said that they came from a fairy underworld and stayed green by living on beans.

Green leaves were a delight. Learned clerks wrote ominously about them signifying sins of the flesh, and preachers warned against the temptations of springtime, but not everyone listened. In May, people carried home branches of hawthorn, with its sweet blossoms. Young couples strolled in the woods, their heads crowned with garlands of ivy. Green Men shared in this symbolism, and in a set of carvings at Weston Longville church, in Norfolk, they surround a young man carrying branches of the May. In fact many Green Men resemble well-dressed youngsters of the period; they are certainly not wild spirits. Their hair-styles, when they can be recognized, are those of fashionable young men of the time.

This Green Man, in Winchester Cathedral, in Hampshire, is a rare example of a full-figure carving and is attacking a lion like some hero of romance. His costume is very dashing, as is usually the case with clothed Green Men: one at Southwell Minster, in Nottinghamshire, wears a jacket with close-cut sleeves, while another at Much Marcle, Herefordshire, has his cloak fastened with a cross-shaped brooch. Green Men keep out the cold with a variety of hoods and comfortable woollen hats.

We think of Green Men in the trees, but often they are surrounded by the leaves of plants. These are frequently conventional, like the acanthus, which was taken from Greek or Roman sculpture and not from life. Among trees, the most common is oak, followed by hawthorn, which is a tree of ordinary human life, of hedgerows not dense forests; oak trees, too, would have been familiar near houses. It seems that the Green Man can belong not only to village and town life but also to the deep woods.

This graceful figure of the Virgin Mary, in Exeter Cathedral, in Devon, at first attracts all of our attention, but then we become aware of the squat little figure of the Green Man trodden beneath her feet, the source of the leafy bower that surrounds her. Green Men often appear in this subservient position on the bases of statues, as do dragons and small goblin figures.

In the chapter house at Southwell Minster, in Nottinghamshire, a series of Green Men is associated with some of the most astonishing leaf sculpture in England. This was produced between 1280 and 1300, when local carvers flirted with the idea of absolute truth to nature. Between the arches of the building, we find hemp, nettle, ivy, bryony, hop, maple, buttercup and rose. The Green Men are a little lumpy by contrast, all the craftsman's attention having been lavished on the leaves around them.

FOREST DEMONS

NOT ALL GREEN MEN are friendly. Some scowl ferociously; others smile, but with such cold eyes that you suspect they are demons. It is true that Green Men do not normally have horns, but in the early Middle Ages these were not always shown on devils either. At Cartmel Priory, Lancashire, the Devil is definitely shown as a Green Man: he has a crown, since he is Prince of this World, three joined-up heads for the Satanic Trinity, and leaves growing from two of them.

These images of wild nature reflect the reality of medieval life. Woods were unsafe places and laws had to be passed to keep them clear and allow for a bowshot on either side of the road. A face glimpsed among the leaves might be a robber or rapist, and not necessarily a human one, for the woods were also reputed to be inhabited by forest fairies with a taste for seduction and violence. Demons could take many forms, including that of walking trees. As late as the seventeenth century, children were frightened with the Man in the Oak. An old chapbook shows him like a Green Man, peeping out from among the branches above a midnight dance of fairies.

It is romantic to think of the Green Man as a spirit of the endless, deep forest, but this simply did not exist in medieval England, which was densely populated and very thinly wooded. At that time there were fewer trees than, for instance, there are in modern France. The word 'forest' meant a hunting ground, not a stretch of trees, and it could be quite barren, like the Forest of Dartmoor. In fact Devon, where the medieval Green Man tradition was to last longest, had less woodland than the outskirts of London.

A rough, bearded face glares down from the vault in Rochester Cathedral, in Kent. In medieval romances, knights who go riding through the forest are often confronted by savage fellows like this: huge, ill-mannered peasants who threaten to fight with them. Real outlaws took advantage of this image, and one of them had the cheek to address his ransom notes from a tree – the Windy Castle of the Greenwood.

With his pointed ears and goat-like face, this Green Man at Worcester Cathedral resembles the classical god Pan. Similarly, there is a carving in the French abbey of Saint-Denis, where the old god Sylvanus is shown as a foliate head. This is not authentic classical tradition, but the sculptor may have been thinking of the sylvani, or forest fairies, who were wont to trick lonely travellers and could take the virginity of an incautious village girl.

Left: This brooding spirit in Coventry Cathedral, in the West Midlands, is the artist's homage to his raw material, for it shows oak leaves carved in seasoned oak wood. The craftsman who created this went on to carve at least two more Green Men of very different character: one at Loversall church, in West Yorkshire, with a gentle and tranquil face, and another in the choir stalls of Lincoln Minster, which looks more like a gap-toothed medieval bandit.

Above: Matted leaves and shaggy hair are almost indistinguishable in this wild face from the church at Brant Broughton, Lincolnshire. Medieval carvings of leaves are often an idealistic notion of foliage, imitated from other carvings rather than nature. The usual practice was to carve stiff leaves, resembling geometrical forms. As far as the sculptors were concerned, the ash, willow, beech, lime and hazel had all grown in vain.

THE TRICKSTER IN THE LEAVES

This smiling couple, a queen and a peasant, ornament the church at Ashby Folville, in Leicestershire. They are peeping heads – looking through a frame of foliage, rather than being part of it. The real Green Lady, with foliage sprouting from her face or mouth, is hardly ever seen (although there is one at Sampford Courtenay church, in Devon). At Kings Nympton church, also in Devon, there is a series of heads: all the male ones are Green Men, but none of the female heads are Green Ladies.

WE ALL LIKE to recognize faces, even faces that are not really there: we see them in clouds, in the shapes of rocks, in leaves on a tree. We also have an instinctive love of green things and nature. The Green Man is special because he fulfils both these requirements, and so it is always a pleasure to find him under a wooden seat, or hidden in an arch, as if we had just triumphed in a private game of hide-and-seek.

People must have felt the same in the Middle Ages, because Green Men are often tucked away in secret places. Those on roof bosses are hardly distinguishable when viewed from the floor below, and if they are carved on misericords, these have to be tilted up for them to be seen at all. Of course, there are some obvious Green Men to be found beside church doors and on chancel screens. No doubt there were once many more, before restorers started tidying up all the odd features of old churches. It would be a mistake to think of carvings like this as the work of some underground movement of mystics or pagans. All church sculpture, pious or grotesque, was commissioned by good Christians.

Even so, it is not easy to give the Green Man an allegorical Christian inter-pretation. All churchgoers knew that a carving of a mermaid stood for Lust and one of a pelican for Compassion, because these interpretations were in the books, but the Green Man is much more a creature of imagination – of trans-formation. Looking at the best foliate heads, you can see that the sculptors have studied the muscles of the face very carefully, exaggerating folds of real skin until they turn into the veins of leaves. Anyone who could read was familiar with transformation stories from the classics, such as Daphne turning into a laurel tree, for they appeared in Ovid's *Metamorphoses*. This was a school textbook, in which you could read commentaries which spelt out a Christian moral for these pagan stories.

Below: From his vantage point in Pershore Abbey, in Worcestershire, this sneering foliate head sticks out his tongue at the world. Tongue-poker faces were originally copied from classical Gorgon masks, which were supposed to ward off evil. It is not certain whether medieval people thought of them in the same way; they have been called 'hanged men', but they are clearly alive. At Bampton church, in Oxfordshire, the tongue-poker wears a king's crown – perhaps as a political satire.

The masons at Ely Cathedral, in Cambridgeshire, had a particular interest in the idea of a face hidden – perhaps with sinister intent – behind the leaves. They must have had a head for heights, for the carving was done on location, 20 metres (70 feet) up. At this shadowy height (Gothic cathedrals are often said to resemble sacred groves) it is not at all clear which ones are foliage and which are animated.

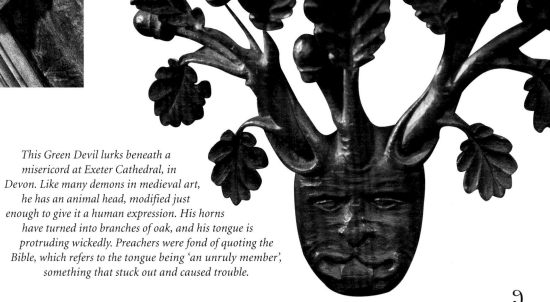

This Green Devil lurks beneath a misericord at Exeter Cathedral, in Devon. Like many demons in medieval art, he has an animal head, modified just enough to give it a human expression. His horns have turned into branches of oak, and his tongue is protruding wickedly. Preachers were fond of quoting the Bible, which refers to the tongue being 'an unruly member', something that stuck out and caused trouble.

Green Men with branches sprouting from their eyes appeared in the 13th century, perhaps as an attempt to copy the foliate heads in which the leaves sprang from the eyebrows or the tear ducts. Later on, the image became popular in Devon, at first in stone carvings, like this one at the church of Ottery St Mary, and then among the roof bosses which were copied from them. It suggests bodily decay rather than renewed life: the tendrils are like the worms that push out of a corpse's eyes on medieval cadaver tombs.

This carving, dated 1483, appears on the keystone of a window in the Chapel of the Nine Altars at Fountains Abbey, in North Yorkshire. The Green Man faces outwards, and there is an angel on the inside. He is in pain, not just because he is being strangled by a twining plant (which looks like honeysuckle) but because he is being squeezed and twisted in the deformation of the arch. In fact the keystone was inserted by masons to prevent the original structure from collapse.

SOME GREEN MEN are frightening, but some are afraid. They are certainly not devils, but they may well be the souls delivered up to them. In the late Middle Ages, after the grim experience of the Black Death, we rarely find a Green Man as wise and venerable as we would like him to be. Instead new, horrific visions gain currency, such as the idea of tendrils sprouting out of his eyes. Foliate heads often play with the signs of old age – leaves originate from the fore-head like wrinkles, or are bunched up into bags under the eyes. This is hard to reconcile with imagery of nature and joy, but after all, an image can express many things, accord-ing to the feelings of the carver. There is no single, arche-typal meaning to which Green Men have to conform.

Sometimes the teeth are made very prominent in the Green Men, perhaps to frighten, or perhaps in a hopeless attempt to bite off some of the encircling foliage. Usually it is the upper teeth that are shown, in a sort of peg-tooth arrangement, like the mouths of giants in an old chapbook. Sometimes the faces seem misshapen. Deformity must have been much more common in the real world than it is now, given the risk of accidents and lack of medical attention for the poor. In the cloisters of Canterbury Cathedral, squinting eyes give the Green Men a horrible leer. Squints are found elsewhere, while sometimes the whole face is lopsided, as if the owner had suffered a stroke.

Medieval people were more worried than us about transformations, such as a man turning into leaves. Their environment was often insecure, so they liked things to fall into definite categories. There is a topsy-turvy world in the margins of manuscripts, full of comic animals which are half one thing and half another, but one senses that sometimes the laughter is forced.

This is certainly a dead man's head, and the tendrils coming from it could be worms as easily as branches. They are like the roots of a churchyard yew, which are said to extend into the mouth of every sleeper in the graves. This roof boss is from the church at South Tawton, Devon. It seems that the West Country, where the Black Death first came ashore, was much possessed by images of death.

LIONS AND DRAGONS

The association of dragons with foliage was made in manuscripts dating from the 10th century. Unlike the cat-mask, which had fallen out of use by the Gothic period, leafy dragons continued to be drawn by book illuminators right up to the arrival of printing. Their serpentine bodies made an ideal framework for capital letters. From the 12th century onwards, the sculptors followed this idea.

GREEN MEN are not the only beings to be closely linked with the plant world. The same image, with leaves growing from the mouth, was also applied by the sculptors to the heads of animals, lions being the most popular. The idea of a lion's head sprouting foliage was a natural development from the cat-mask which early manuscripts had used as a decorative ornament, and which had been taken up by stonemasons in the twelfth century at the same time as the Green Man.

Throughout the Middle Ages, lions were the most common form of animal head, just as they had been in classical art. Lions' heads were made into spouts for fountains or held rings in their teeth to act as door knockers. They were as good as human heads, or better, if a round design was needed on something like a roof boss. Some other animals were shown with foliage; there is a Green Dog at St Mary Redcliffe, Bristol, and a wolf at Tewkesbury Abbey, Gloucestershire – but lions were the favourite.

Unlike Green Men, who are ignored by contemporary documents, the lion's symbolism is carefully explained for us. Unfortunately, this is contradictory: sometimes he is like Christ, but sometimes he is the Devil who goes about as a roaring lion, seeking whomsoever he may devour. There is no uncertainty about dragons, which are always diabolical; the idea that they represent the energies of the earth is an entirely modern one. Artists took delight in carving or painting Green Dragons. Sometimes the green growth comes out of their mouths and sometimes their tails also mutate into twirling branches. Some dragons, like the graceful ones circling the font at Studham church in Bedfordshire, are intended to represent the Devil, driven out of the font by the powers of baptism. Others seem to have no moral purpose at all.

In the West Country and on the Welsh border, the 15th-century carvers of chancel screens made great play with the image of dragons biting at grapes. This dragon in the church of Sampford Courtenay, Devon, is growing into vines at one end and eating them at the other, so that he devours himself. Dragons and foliage were interchangeable: some carved heads, which look like Green Men at a distance, turn out on closer inspection to be disgorging snakes or dragons.

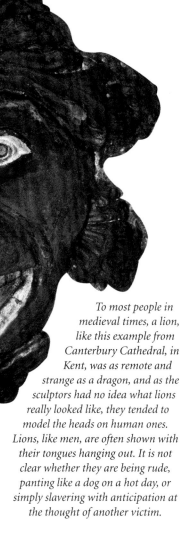

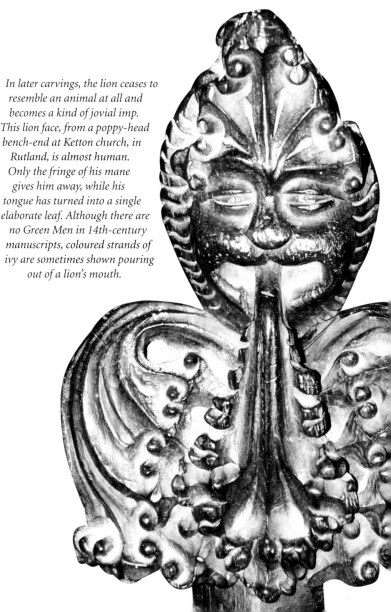

In later carvings, the lion ceases to resemble an animal at all and becomes a kind of jovial imp. This lion face, from a poppy-head bench-end at Ketton church, in Rutland, is almost human. Only the fringe of his mane gives him away, while his tongue has turned into a single elaborate leaf. Although there are no Green Men in 14th-century manuscripts, coloured strands of ivy are sometimes shown pouring out of a lion's mouth.

To most people in medieval times, a lion, like this example from Canterbury Cathedral, in Kent, was as remote and strange as a dragon, and as the sculptors had no idea what lions really looked like, they tended to model the heads on human ones. Lions, like men, are often shown with their tongues hanging out. It is not clear whether they are being rude, panting like a dog on a hot day, or simply slavering with anticipation at the thought of another victim.

THE 'GREEN MAN' is not the original name of this character, but a scholar's convention. This is confusing because, in popular traditions of the Middle Ages, and later, there is a character who really is called a Green Man. He is a giant who lives in the woods, wearing no clothes, apart from a suit of leaves, and whose hair and beard are long and shaggy. He is a version of the Wild Man, a figure of primal savagery who haunted the medieval imagination.

Leaf disguises, imitating the Wild Man, were incorporated in later folk customs. They are still popular in Germany and in Switzerland, where a *wilde mann*, dressed in green and carrying an uprooted tree, parades through the city of Basle every January. There has never been an English custom quite like this, but there are several events, such as the Garland ceremony of Castleton, Derbyshire, in which the leading character wears a hollow frame covered with leaves and flowers. The phrase 'Jack-in-the-Green' is used in English sources to describe someone dressed up in this way.

The Wild Man and the Green/Wild Man are creatures of the forest, living in hollow trees and carrying leaves and branches, but they are very different from the Green Man of church carvings, who is often a dapper young fellow, not monstrous at all. The fourteenth-century poem *Sir Gawain and the Green Knight* tells of a giant figure who is green all over, and who lives in a mysterious castle in the forest. He is not savage, but courteous and morally superior to King Arthur's knights. Although he is a quite different figure from the Green Man, he seems to embody very similar ideas. Later poems and ballads celebrate Robin Hood, a handsome, upright hero who nevertheless lives an outlaw's life in the woods and dresses in green.

The Wild Man was a popular figure in medieval decorations, such as this 15th-century Swiss tapestry. People recognized him because he was a favourite disguise for figures in pageants. A suit of leaves was easy to construct, and a grotesque mask could be fixed over the guiser's face. Because everybody knew they were rough, animal types, these Wild Men were used to clear crowds out of the way before the main procession came.

Below: There are many public houses called 'The Green Man', such as this one at Kings Stag, Dorset, and the oldest have borne this name since the 17th century. The earliest signs show the Wild Man, and some later ones a Jack-in-the-Green or a forester, but as a result of recent interest, several have been repainted with our kind of Green Man – the foliate head.

Above: It is not certain what the earliest kind of Jack-in-the-Green was, but by the 18th century, the name had come to mean a chimney sweep who fitted himself into a conical framework of foliage and danced with his friends on May Day morning, collecting contributions from passers-by. The custom began in London – this picture shows a scene in Upper Lisson Street – but spread into the countryside, becoming part of May Day celebrations.

GREEN MAN

FREE HOUSE

This Green Man, with his fertile moustache, is set in the Gage gates at Tewkesbury Abbey, in Gloucestershire. The gates were made in 1734, during the great age of wrought iron; about the same time, Green Men were being fitted into screens in St Paul's Cathedral, London, and in St Mary Redcliffe, Bristol. Their pugnacious masculinity derives from Renaissance decorative art – a quite different world from that of the medieval sculptures found in the same buildings.

Although this head was carved in 1534, it is still in medieval style, but the opposed mermen above it are more Renaissance. The carver who provided this bench-end for Crowcombe church, in Somerset, was a very imitative fellow: he copied one of his dragons from a misericord at Bristol Cathedral, and that in turn was copied from an early printed book. People like to find secret meanings in these images, but they are often just a carver's fancy.

THROUGHOUT the Middle Ages, the image of the Green Man evolved into different forms which were often quite different from their prototype in Ancient Rome. In the sixteenth century, however, there was a conscious attempt to return to classical art – not just the high art of heroic statues, but the ornamental details as well. The Roman building known as 'Nero's Golden House' was rediscovered by scholars, and its grotesque little men, peeping out of foliage, became popular, first in the borders of illuminated or early printed books and then in decorative sculpture.

Craftsmen learned to produce these ornamental leaf masks along with other Renaissance detail and did not give them much personality. Sprouting heads, however, continued to be carved in the medieval style in a few places, especially tombs, because the Green Man had become associated with thoughts of death and resurrection. The dark growth of a churchyard's ivy and yew remind us of death because the plants so obviously care nothing for the people below – and yet they are also like a green resurrection. Stories of a tree or flower which grows from a corpse are very old. In one Christian legend, the tree from which the True Cross was fashioned grew originally out of the grave of Adam. The ballad *True William and Fair Margaret* tells how two unhappy lovers die and are buried in the churchyard: a rose and a briar grow from their graves and entwine over the church.

Following this tradition, the architect William Burges (1827–81) described the foliate heads which he included in the fantastical Castell Coch, near Cardiff, as *Life and Death in Nature*. Other Victorians took a more robust view: Decimus Burton (1800–81) placed Green Men on the gates of the Royal Botanical Gardens at Kew to remind visitors that nature was not just a source of spiritual regeneration but also a useful resource for the British Empire.

Seen in profile at Lacock Abbey, in Wiltshire, this Green Man seems to have a cheerful outlook on life although he is decorating a tomb. Some monuments feature a skull sprouting foliage, an idea which first appeared in medieval Scotland, at Glasgow Cathedral and Rosslyn Chapel. Later, in the 18th century, Green Skulls became common on Scottish gravestones, where they were intended to remind mourners that all flesh is grass and that we wither like the flowers of the field.

Leaf masks in the classical style were widely imitated. Some presented a real challenge to the sculptor: in this carving at Westminster Abbey, London, the leaves have been twisted to create the form of a face, with eyes, nose and mouth, but without ceasing to be anything but leaves. This game of substituting plant life for human life was perfected by the Italian artist Arcimboldo, who painted a series of heads consisting of artfully arranged fruits and vegetables.

17

IN THE 1930s, two writers – Lady Raglan and C.J.P. Cave – came independently to believe that the Green Man, with whom they had become familiar in their study of medieval church carvings, was not just a fantastic figure. They decided that he must be a depiction of young men dressed up in a framework of leaves, like the Jack-in-the-Green of the eighteenth century, to celebrate May Day. This is almost certainly untrue because there are many pictures of May Day revellers in the Middle Ages, and none of them show a costume like this. It was invented centuries after the Green Man had been created in the imagination of artists and sculptors.

Other writers followed them in identifying the Green Man as something ancient, pagan and magical. They drew together characters as different as the English John Barleycorn, with his beard of bristling barley, and the Greek Dionysus, with his hair wreathed in vines. From these they created a composite god, who had never existed, but whose legend seemed strangely familiar. He was born at the turn of the year and grew up with the fresh greenery. He took a lover in spring and was killed at the waning of the year, only to rise again with the new leaves.

People from other religious backgrounds were also drawn to rediscover spirituality in nature, especially in their relationships with trees. Images which enriched this view were brought into the fantasy world of millions by the Christian writer J.R.R. Tolkien in *The Lord of the Rings*, where the immensely old and powerful Ents, half-way between men and trees, lead lives of quiet wisdom in the deep forest.

Modern movements, both ecological and pagan, needed an emblem to symbolize the unity of man and nature. They found what they needed in this mysterious old church carving. The Green Man began as a grotesque: it is we who have made him into a god.

Crooked, whispering trees watch over Peer Gynt in Arthur Rackham's illustration of this Norwegian tale. Rackham specialized in drawing this kind of animated wildwood, and the first scholars to revive interest in the Green Man had been raised on picture books full of these haunting images. Theirs was also the generation that saw the first campaigns to save trees, not as useful landmarks or sources of timber, but as living beings, perhaps wiser than the people who sought to cut them down.

Many artists are rediscovering the Green Man, not necessarily as a spiritual figure, but as a way of exploring the boundless vitality of nature. Wooden effigies of Green Men can be found, half-hidden among the trees, like this one from Stewart Park, in Middlesbrough. At the commercial level there are now many terracotta or concrete plaques with foliate heads, patient and noble in expression, which can bring the power of nature into your garden.

Below: The Green Man, as imagined by the artist Mary Fedden, attends a typically English harvest festival. In the half-century since his rediscovery, the Green Man has ceased to be just an antiquarian curiosity, becoming instead an instantly recognizable personality, part of the imaginative life of millions of people. If he had not already existed as a church carving, something very like him would have been invented to embody the spirit of nature.

Sporting the antlers of the Horned God, a festive Green Man presides over the May Day celebrations at Clun, Shropshire. Dancers disguised as Wild Men or Green Men perform in several of today's Morris sides. Ritual figures like this seem to be re-enacting old traditions that have been forgotten, or perhaps suppressed during a less spiritual age. It might be truer to say that they are using the shaping power of imagination to create a new, green religion.

19

BRITAIN IS rich in medieval buildings, from great cathedrals to parish churches, and Green Men may be found lurking in many of them. The best places to look for them are on the roof bosses, the capitals at the top of columns, bench-ends and the hinged wooden seats known as misericords. The list below gives fuller details of the places mentioned in the book, as well as other sites where outstanding examples can be found.

ENGLAND
Bedfordshire
Studham: *St Mary* (see p.12)
Berkshire
Windsor: *St George's Chapel*
Bristol
Bristol: *Bristol Cathedral* (see p.16); *St Mary Redcliffe* (see pp.12, 16)
Cambridgeshire
Cambridge: *Kings College*
Ely: *Ely Cathedral* (see p.9)
Cheshire
Chester: *Chester Cathedral*
Nantwich: *St Mary*
Devon
Exeter: *Exeter Cathedral* (see inside front cover, pp.5, 9)
Kings Nympton: *St James* (see p.8)
Ottery St Mary: *St Mary* (see p.10)
Sampford Courtenay: *St Andrew* (see pp.8, 13)
South Tawton: *St Andrew* (see p.11)
Tawstock: *St Peter*
Dorset
Sherborne: *Sherborne Abbey*
East Riding of Yorkshire
Beverley: *Beverley Minster*
Gloucestershire
Gloucester: *Gloucester Cathedral*
Tewkesbury: *Tewkesbury Abbey* (see pp.12, 16)
Hampshire
Romsey: *Romsey Abbey*
Winchester: *Winchester Cathedral* (see p.5)
Herefordshire
Holt: *St Martin*
Kilpeck: *Sts Mary & David* (see p.2)
Leominster: *Leominster Priory*
Much Marcle: *St Bartholomew* (see p.5)

Hertfordshire
St Albans: *St Albans Cathedral*
Kent
Canterbury: *Canterbury Cathedral* (see pp.2, 11, 13, 21)
Rochester: *Rochester Cathedral* (see p.6)
Lancashire
Cartmel: *Cartmel Priory* (see p.6)
Leicestershire
Ashby Folville: *St Mary's* (see p.8)
Lincolnshire
Boston: *St Botolph*
Brant Broughton: *St Helen* (see p.7)
Lincoln: *Lincoln Minster* (see p.7)
London
St Paul's Cathedral (see pp.16, 20–21)
Westminster Abbey (see p.17)
Norfolk
King's Lynn: *St Margaret*
Norwich: *Norwich Cathedral* (see p.1)
Weston Longville: *All Saints* (see p.4)

North Yorkshire
Near Ripon: *Fountains Abbey* (see p.10)
York: *York Minster* (see p.20)
Nottinghamshire
Southwell: *Southwell Minster* (see p.5)
Oxfordshire
Bampton: *St Mary* (see p.9)
Dorchester: *Dorchester Abbey*
Oxford: *Christ Church*
Rutland
Ketton: *St Mary* (see p.13)
Shropshire
Ludlow: *St Lawrence*
Somerset
Crowcombe: *Holy Trinity* (see p.16)
Lullington: *All Saints* (see p.3)
Wells: *Wells Cathedral* (see p.3)
Staffordshire
Lichfield: *Lichfield Cathedral*
Suffolk
Sudbury: *St Peter*
Surrey
Richmond: *Royal Botanical Gardens, Kew* (see p.16)
Warwickshire
Stratford-on-Avon: *Holy Trinity*
West Midlands
Coventry: *Coventry Cathedral* (see p.7)